D1300609

SUPER SANDCASTLE
State Stories

MISSY THE SHOW-ME MULE

~ A Story About Missouri ~

Written by Nancy Tuminelly

Illustrated by Bob Doucet

Consulting Editor, Diane Craig, M.A./Reading Specialist

A Division of ABDO
ABDO
Publishing Company

visit us at www.abdopublishing.com

Published by ABDO Publishing Company, a division of ABDO, P.O. Box 398166, Minneapolis, Minnesota 55439. Copyright © 2011 by Abdo Consulting Group, Inc. International copyrights reserved in all countries. No part of this book may be reproduced in any form without written permission from the publisher. Super SandCastle™ is a trademark and logo of ABDO Publishing Company.

Printed in the United States of America, North Mankato, Minnesota
112010
012011

 PRINTED ON RECYCLED PAPER

Editor: Liz Salzmann
Content Developer: Nancy Tuminelly
Cover and Interior Design: Anders Hanson, Mighty Media
Production: Colleen Dolphin, Oona Gaarder-Juntti, Mighty Media
Photo Credits: Americasroof, Andrew Balet, Blambo, ChurchillMemorial, Debi Boughton, Fantastic Caverns, iStockphoto (Amit Erez, Dale Morrow), Robert Lawton, Ryan Mooney, Nationalparks, One Mile Up, Quarter-dollar coin image from the United States Mint, Shutterstock

Library of Congress Cataloging-in-Publication Data

Tuminelly, Nancy, 1952-
  Missy the show-me mule : a story about Missouri / Nancy Tuminelly ; illustrated by Bob Doucet.
    p. cm. -- (Fact & fable: state stories)
  ISBN 978-1-61714-682-4
  1. Missouri--Juvenile literature. I. Doucet, Bob, ill. II. Title.
  F466.3.T86 2011
  977.8--dc22
                          2010022172

Super SandCastle™ books are created by a team of professional educators, reading specialists, and content developers around five essential components—phonemic awareness, phonics, vocabulary, text comprehension, and fluency—to assist young readers as they develop reading skills and strategies and increase their general knowledge. All books are written, reviewed, and leveled for guided reading, early reading intervention, and Accelerated Reader® programs for use in shared, guided, and independent reading and writing activities to support a balanced approach to literacy instruction.

TABLE OF CONTENTS

Pony Express
(pg. 18)

Mississippi River
(pg. 14)

St. Joseph

Grand River

Hannibal

bluebird
(pg. 11)

Kansas City

Jefferson City

Missouri River

Nelson-Atkins
Museum of Art
(pg. 17)

channel catfish
(pg. 9)

Osage River

Gateway Arch
(pg. 12)

St. Louis

Lake of
the Ozarks
(pg. 8)

MISSOURI

Mississippi River

Springfield

Missouri Bootheel
(pg. 5)

mule
(pg. 4)

LEGEND

⭐ CAPITAL   ◎ STORY START

◯ CITY   - - - STORY PATH

RIVER   ✦ STORY END

3

Mule

The mule is the Missouri state animal. It comes from a male donkey and a female horse. Mules are strong work animals. Farmers use mules in the fields instead of horses. Mules are curious and very smart.

MISSY THE SHOW-ME MULE

issy lives on a farm in the Missouri Bootheel. She is **stubborn** and unfriendly most of the time. Missy thinks everything is "BORING." Others try to tell her about things that aren't boring. Missy just stomps her hoof and says, "Show me!"

Her family and friends don't like the way she acts. No one wants to be around her.

Missy's family is going on a trip to St. Joseph. Of course, she says it will be BORING. As they leave, Missy closes her eyes and drifts into dreamland.

Out of the clouds appears Mighty Mo, the "Show Me" superhero.

Bootheel

The southeastern corner of Missouri is called the Bootheel. It is shaped like the heel of a boot! It is mostly farmland. The farmers there grow **soybeans**, rice, cotton, and melons.

5

Springfield

Springfield is the third-largest city in Missouri. The Springfield Cardinals play at Hammons Field. They are a minor league baseball team. Other fun things to see are Bass Pro Shops World and Wilson's Creek National Battlefield.

"Did you know caves are really cool?" asks Mighty Mo.

"Show me! I don't believe it," says Missy.

In Springfield, Missy sees a baseball field. "I'd rather go to a baseball game," she says.

"BORING!" kids Mo. "We can do that next time. Besides, you just said to show you a cave."

Missy is afraid of caves. She doesn't like the dark.

"We'll ride the **tram** through Fantastic Caverns. It's on a lighted path." Mighty Mo says.

"Look at those **stalactites** and **stalagmites**!" yells Mo.

"They're okay," Missy says. She really likes the cave but doesn't want Mo to know.

"Okay, let's go to The Lake next. It's so much fun!" says Mo.

Fantastic Caverns

Fantastic Caverns is the only ride-through cave in the United States. Visitors can enjoy the cave without walking or climbing. The tram follows an old underground river. The path is lighted to show all of the natural wonders.

7

Lake of the Ozarks

"The Lake" is the nickname for Lake of the Ozarks. It is one of the largest man-made lakes in the world. It was formed in 1931 when Bagnell Dam was built. Many people like to boat and fish on The Lake.

"So, show me what's fun here!" says Missy. She was afraid of water too.

When they cross Bagnell Dam, she peeks out of one eye. The Lake is on one side. The Osage River is on the other side.

"Who wants to have fun?" says a voice from the Lake. It's Charlie, the channel catfish.

"Charlie, meet Missy. She thinks everything is BORING," says Mighty Mo. He winks at Charlie.

They spend the day boating and swimming.

"Do you like to fish?" asks Charlie. "I always catch the most!" he brags. "That's why I'm so big!"

"It was a pretty good day," says Missy. She didn't want them to know she had fun. "Now what?"

Channel Catfish

The channel catfish is the state fish of Missouri. It is a thin fish with a forked tail. It uses its **whiskers** to find food, not its eyes. Channel catfish can be 36 inches (91 cm) long. They can weigh up to 50 pounds (23 kg).

Jefferson City

Jefferson City is the Missouri state capital. It is located on the Missouri River. It was named for Thomas Jefferson, the third president of the United States. There are many government buildings here. Lincoln University was founded here in 1866 at the end of the Civil War.

"There's so much to see at the capital!" says Mighty Mo.

"Yeah, right. Show me," says Missy. She tries not to show she is enjoying their adventure.

They tour the Missouri State **Museum** in the Capitol Building. Then they wander through the Lewis and Clark Trailhead Plaza. It has **statues** and fountains.

They see flowering dogwood trees at the Governor's Mansion. "Those flowers look like crosses," says Missy.

"You're right!" says a voice from a tree. They look up and see a brightly colored bluebird.

"Hi Bert," says Mighty Mo. "This is Missy. She says everything is BORING."

"Maybe we should show her St. Louis," suggests Bert.

"So, show me," Missy says with a little smile.

Bluebird

The bluebird is the Missouri state bird. It is a songbird. It has an orange chest and blue head, wings, and tail. It eats **insects** and small fruits or berries.

11

St. Louis

St. Louis is the second-largest city in the state. It is nicknamed "Gateway to the West." In the 1800s, many settlers stopped there on their way west. The Gateway Arch was built in the 1960s. A **tram** inside the arch takes people to the top. There are windows with wonderful views.

"Let's go up in the Gateway Arch. We can see for miles!" says Mighty Mo.

Missy is also afraid of heights. But before she can say anything, they are at the top. They look out across the big city and the Mississippi River.

"Let's get a snack and then hop on a riverboat!" says Bert. "St. Louis has the best **toasted ravioli**. We can get some on the way."

"These taste great!" says Missy.

Mo and Missy hop on a riverboat. It paddles up the Mississippi River. Missy has so much fun she forgets she is afraid of the water.

Toasted Ravioli Recipe

½ cup Italian seasoned fine bread crumbs

2 tablespoons Parmesan cheese, grated

1 large egg, slightly beaten

1 package frozen cheese ravioli, thawed

3 tablespoons olive oil

1 jar marinara sauce, warmed

Mix bread crumbs and cheese in a medium bowl. Dip each ravioli in the egg. Then dip them in the bread crumb mixture. Coat both sides well. Heat the olive oil in a large frying pan on medium-high heat. Add the ravioli. Cook them 2 to 3 minutes on each side until golden brown. Dip them in marinara sauce. Enjoy!

Mighty Mo, Bert, and Missy finish their toasted ravioli.

"Time to head up the river, Missy," says Mo.

"You two have fun. I'm too full to fly" says Bert.

"Bye, Bert!" says Missy.

Toasted Ravioli

Toasted ravioli are breaded, deep-fried ravioli. They are served with marinara sauce and Parmesan cheese. Toasted ravioli are popular in St. Louis, especially in Italian neighborhoods. Locals call them T-ravs!

Mississippi River

The Mississippi River is called "The Mighty Mississippi." It is 2,350 miles (3,782 km) long. It begins at Lake Itasca, Minnesota. It ends in Louisiana at the Gulf of Mexico.

"Look!" says Missy. She points to some kids on a **raft**. They are floating down the river by the shore.

"They look like Tom Sawyer, Huckleberry Finn, and Becky Thatcher," says Mo.

"Come on, I'll show you," says Mo. They go to the Mark Twain **Museum** in Hannibal.

Missy learns about Mark Twain. He wrote about growing up in Hannibal on the Mississippi. Many things in the town are named after the author and his book characters.

"I'll show you some water that won't scare you," says Mo.

Hannibal

Hannibal is on the Mississippi River. The famous author Mark Twain grew up there. His book, *The Adventures of Tom Sawyer*, is about a boy and his friends growing up on the river. Mark Twain's childhood home is now a museum.

Kansas City

Kansas City is the largest city in Missouri. It is called the "City of Fountains." It is home of the Kansas City Chiefs football team and the Kansas City Royals baseball team. Kansas City is known for great **jazz** and blues music and **barbecue**.

"OK, show me!" says Missy. Pretty soon they are in Kansas City. They see beautiful fountains at Country Club Plaza and along the roads.

"How about some barbecue?" asks Mighty Mo.

"Yum! Show me!" says Missy. They went to B.B.'s Lawnside BBQ for ribs and music.

"I haven't heard you say anything is BORING in a while," says Mo.

They walk over to the Nelson-Atkins **Museum** of Art.
"Now its time for a little art," says Mo.

"I'm ready! Show me!" says Missy. "What's that?"

"That's a giant **badminton** birdie," answers Mo.

"Does Bert know that birdie?" asks Missy.

"No," says Mo laughing. "Let me show you the mummies inside."

All of a sudden, Mo disappears!

"Mo! Where are you?" yells Missy.

Nelson-Atkins Museum of Art

The Nelson-Atkins Museum of Art has more than 34,000 pieces of art. Some of it is on the museum's lawn! These outdoor pieces belong to the Kansas City Sculpture Park. The park is famous for it's huge sculptures of badminton birdies!

17

St. Joseph

St. Joseph is a historic city on the Missouri River. It has many beautiful old buildings. The Pony Express began there in 1860. The Pony Express carried mail between St. Joseph and Sacramento, California.

Missy wakes up in the car as they arrive in St. Joseph. She says, "Show me all the fun things here!"

"Hold your horses, Missy! What's the rush?" asks Auntie Mame. "I'll show you where the Pony Express got its start."

For a minute, Missy thought Auntie Mame sounded like Mighty Mo!

"Show me MORE!" exclaims Missy.

Next they visit the house where Jesse James lived. Missy realizes there are interesting things everywhere. Nothing is boring!

She tells her family, "There are lots of wonderful things I can show you on the way home!"

Out of the corner of her eye Missy sees Mighty Mo smiling at her.

"Show me!" he says.

THE END

Jesse James

Jesse James was a famous **outlaw**. He was in several gangs that robbed banks and trains. In 1881, Jesse moved to St. Joseph with his family. A member of his gang shot him there in 1882.

19

MISSOURI AT A GLANCE

Abbreviation: MO

Capital: Jefferson City

Largest city: Kansas City

Statehood: August 10, 1821 (24th state)

Area: 69,704 square miles (180,532 sq km) (20th-largest state)

Nickname: Show-Me State

Motto: Sallus populi suprema lex esto — The welfare of the people shall be the supreme law

State flower: white hawthorn

State tree: flowering dogwood

State bird: bluebird

State fish: channel catfish

State animal: Missouri mule

State insect: honeybee

State song: "Missouri Waltz"

STATE SEAL

STATE FLAG

STATE QUARTER

The Missouri quarter shows Lewis and Clark on the Missouri River. They began their trip in 1804 and returned to St. Louis in 1806. The Gateway Arch is in the background. "Corps of Discovery 1804–2004" refers to the 200-year anniversary of the Lewis and Clark Expedition.

WHAT DO YOU KNOW?

How well do you remember the story? Match the pictures to the questions below! Then check your answers at the bottom of the page!

 **a.** Fantastic Caverns

 **b.** bluebird

 **c.** St. Joseph

 **d.** Charlie the channel catfish

 **e.** toasted ravioli

 **f.** Mighty Mo

1. Who is the "Show Me" superhero?

2. Where does Missy see **stalactites** and **stalagmites**?

3. Who does Missy meet at Lake of the Ozarks?

4. What kind of animal is Bert?

5. What does Missy eat in St. Louis?

6. Where is Missy when she wakes up?

What to Do in Missouri

1 **See an Ozark Opry show**

Dolly Parton's Dixie Stampede Dinner Attraction, Branson

2 **Visit a museum!**

National Historical Cookie Cutter Museum, Joplin

3 **Learn about Harry S. Truman**

Harry S. Truman Historic Site, Independence

4 **See a Civil War battlefield**

Battle of Kirksville battlefield, Kirksville

5 **Ride your bike along a railroad line**

Katy Trail, Boonville

6 **Walk through part of the Berlin Wall**

Breakthrough—The Cold War Memorial, Fulton

7 **Go on a historic walking tour**

Historic Walking Tour of Rolla, Rolla

8 **Go camping and hiking**

Hawn State Park, St. Genevieve

Iowa

Nebraska

Illinois

Kansas

⬜3

⬜5 ⬜6

★ Jefferson City

MISSOURI

⬜7

⬜8

Kentucky

⬜2

⬜1

Oklahoma

Arkansas

Tennessee

⬜4

23

GLOSSARY

badminton – a game in which the players use rackets to hit a shuttlecock or birdie over a high net.

barbecue – meat seasoned with a spicy, tangy sauce and cooked over a fire or hot charcoal. *Barbecue* is sometimes written *BBQ*.

insect – a small creature with two or four wings, six legs, and a body with sections.

jazz – an American style of music in which musicians often make up the tune as they play.

museum – a place where artistic, scientific, or historic things are cared for, studied, and displayed.

outlaw – a criminal, such as a robber, who runs and hides from the police.

raft – a flat boat or mat used to float on water.

ravioli – a type of pasta shaped into pockets and filled with meat or cheese.

soybean – a type of seed grown for food and oil.

stalactite – a pointy rock that hangs down from the roof of a cave.

stalagmite – a pointy rock that sticks up from the floor of a cave.

statue – a model of something made out of a solid material such as wood, metal, or stone.

stubborn – wanting to have one's own way and being unwilling to change or give in.

toasted – cooked so it is crispy.

tram – a small train that travels on rails or an overhead cable.

whisker – one of the long hairs around the mouth of an animal.

DATE DUE

			PRINTED IN U.S.A.